This is the true story of Lakota (la-COAT-ah),
the gentle wolf who braved bullying.

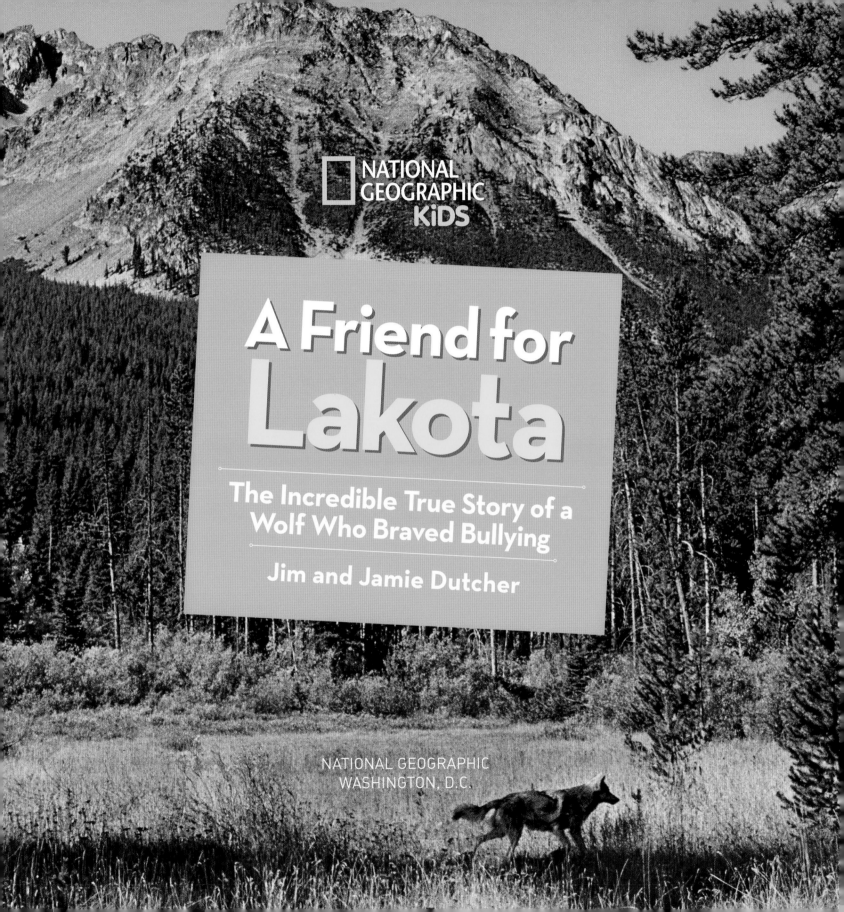

NATIONAL GEOGRAPHIC KiDS

A Friend for Lakota

The Incredible True Story of a Wolf Who Braved Bullying

Jim and Jamie Dutcher

NATIONAL GEOGRAPHIC
WASHINGTON, D.C.

Spring blooms over the Sawtooth Mountains of Idaho. Wildflowers splash patches of bright colors across the meadows. And a young wolf pup, Lakota, rolls in the fresh green grass.

Lakota spends all day playing. He turns every rock, log, and stick into a toy. His days are simple and fun.

But in a wolf's world, things can change quickly.

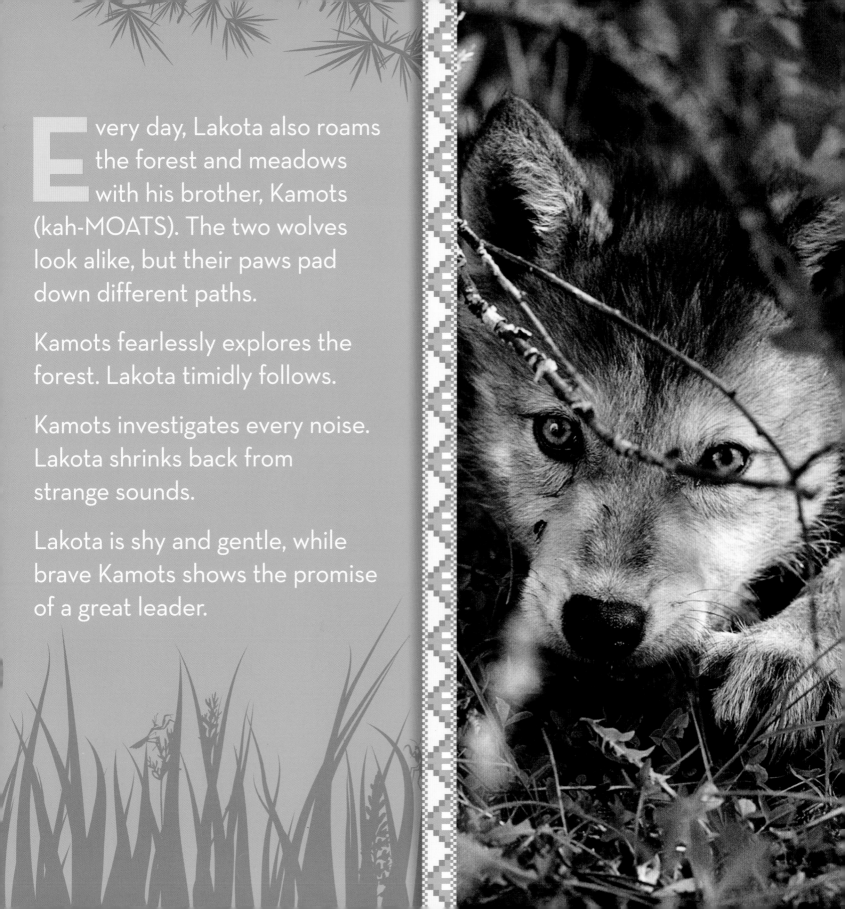

Every day, Lakota also roams the forest and meadows with his brother, Kamots (kah-MOATS). The two wolves look alike, but their paws pad down different paths.

Kamots fearlessly explores the forest. Lakota timidly follows.

Kamots investigates every noise. Lakota shrinks back from strange sounds.

Lakota is shy and gentle, while brave Kamots shows the promise of a great leader.

Soon, the first snowflakes fall over the mountains, covering the wolves' world in a thick white blanket. Lakota and Kamots grow. Their lean legs stretch tall. And their fur coats thicken to keep them warm in the freezing air.

As winter melts into spring, three new wolves join the brothers. Now instead of just two, they are a family of five. They are now a wolf pack.

Every member of Lakota's pack has a job to do. Kamots quickly rises to be a strong leader. Amani (uh-MAH-knee) causes trouble, while Matsi (MOT-zee) keeps the peace.

Suddenly, Kamots lifts his head and lets out a long *arrooooooooo!* The rest of the pack gathers around him and joins in—their howls a chorus echoing in the mountains.

By the following winter, Lakota, too, settles into his position in the family. Gentle Lakota never challenges the other wolves. His job is to help everyone play, to get along. Easy to do—when all the wolves seem to be in a good mood.

But one snowy day, as pack members chase one another, something happens. The wolves suddenly heap on top of Lakota. They snarl in his face!

Lakota whimpers and drops to the ground, as low as he can go, waiting timidly for the pile of wolves to retreat.

Just a few days later, it happens again. And then again. Before long, Lakota is being picked on all the time. One wolf nips at his tail; another jumps on him. Another pulls on his fur.

Matsi doesn't join the other wolves. He doesn't jump on Lakota. He never pulls on his fur. But he watches.

One day Amani confronts Lakota in full view of the others. He growls deeply. Then, he charges!

Lakota drops to the ground and, trembling, tries to crawl away.

But all of a sudden, in a whirl of fur, Matsi jumps between Amani and Lakota, letting out a loud snarl. Amani skids to a stop and backs off.

There will be no picking on Lakota today.

Soon Matsi and Lakota become the best of friends.

In summer, they play tag and roll in the long grass. In fall, they race through the aspen leaves that float down from the trees. In winter, they pounce on a stream's newly formed ice to hear it pop and crack under their feet.

The other wolves don't bother Lakota when he is with Matsi. Matsi won't allow it.

Sometimes Matsi and Lakota wander off, away from the others. With just his friend, Lakota can finally run, jump, and chase—like all wolves do.

Lakota jumps on Matsi's back, his tail happily wagging back and forth. He whines at Matsi, inviting him to play. And Matsi always plays back. He seems to know this is what his friend needs.

As Lakota grows older and new pups join the pack, his confidence seems to soar. In time, the other wolves leave him alone. They stop picking on him.

Lakota and Matsi stay best friends.

Still, Lakota never seems to forget his past. He was once at the bottom of the pile. But there was the friendship that Matsi gave him when no one else would.

Sometimes the other wolves pick on the young ones.

But Lakota never does.

Lakota's home
and where wolves live in North America

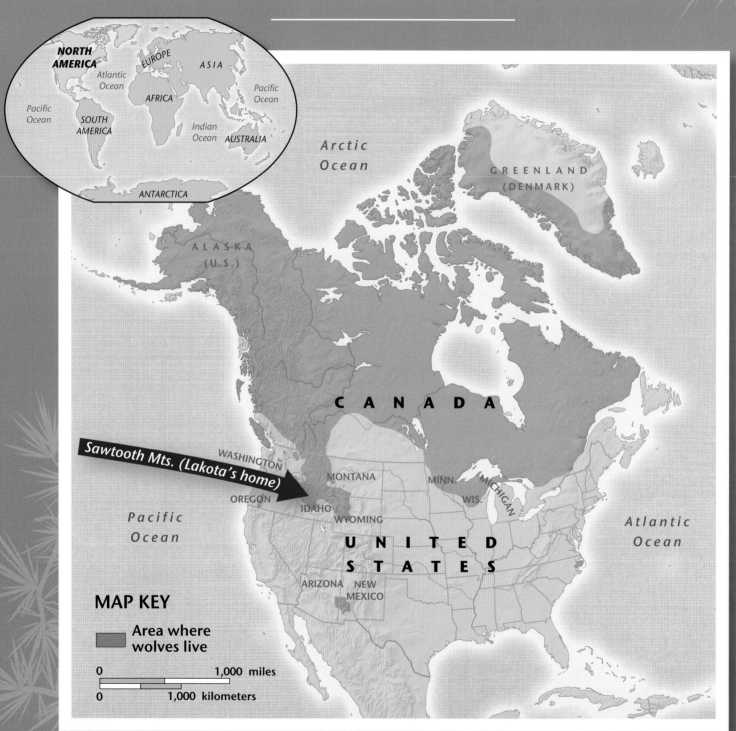

NORTH AMERICA
EUROPE
ASIA
Atlantic Ocean
AFRICA
Pacific Ocean
Pacific Ocean
SOUTH AMERICA
Indian Ocean
AUSTRALIA
ANTARCTICA

Arctic Ocean

GREENLAND (DENMARK)

ALASKA (U.S.)

CANADA

Sawtooth Mts. (Lakota's home)

WASHINGTON

MONTANA

MINN.

MICHIGAN

WIS.

OREGON

IDAHO

WYOMING

Pacific Ocean

Atlantic Ocean

UNITED STATES

ARIZONA

NEW MEXICO

MAP KEY

Area where wolves live

0   1,000 miles

0   1,000 kilometers

All about Lakota and gray wolves

- Wolves are social mammals like humans. They live in family groups known as packs. Wolf pups drink milk from their mothers.

- Dogs descended from wolves between 12,000 and 30,000 years ago. Dogs and wolves communicate similarly. Both wag their tails, growl, yip, and howl.

- Wolves are carnivores, or meat-eaters. Some of their favorite foods are deer, bison, elk, and moose. But they'll also eat smaller animals if their preferred prey is hard to find. A wolf can eat up to 20 pounds (9 kg) of food in one sitting.

- Gray wolves live in Alaska, U.S.A.; Canada; and parts of Europe and Asia. They were nearly hunted to extinction in most of the United States and Europe. In some places, such as Yellowstone National Park in the United States, wolves have been reintroduced successfully. But all wolves today still face many threats to their survival.

- Wolves vary in size, usually depending on where they live and what they hunt. Wolves in northern regions, like Lakota and his pack in Idaho, U.S.A., are typically larger, because they feed on big animals such as elk and deer. Wolves in southern locations, such as Arizona, U.S.A., hunt deer and rabbits, and can be a little smaller. Females usually weigh 60 to 75 pounds (27 to 34 kg). Males are larger and weigh up to 130 pounds (59 kg).

FUN FACT: "Lakota" is a Native American word. In the Lakota Sioux language, it means "friends" or "allies."

A note from the authors

After filming and photographing many of the pack's incredible stories, our U.S. government permits for the project expired, so we moved the wolves to protected land on the Nez Perce Reservation in northern Idaho. There, Lakota, Matsi, Kamots, and the other wolves peacefully lived out the rest of their lives.

We know there is still a lot of work to do to save this endangered species. So, in 2005 we put down our camera gear and started Living With Wolves, a nonprofit organization dedicated to showing the world the true nature of these amazing animals. By sharing powerful stories such as Lakota's, we want to enrich people's understanding of wolves, which we hope will help wild wolves in packs all over the world.

—Jim and Jamie Dutcher

We built our wolf camp close to the pack so we could observe the wolves in their natural environment.

Not many people can say they've lived with wolves. But for six years, in a tented camp deep in the Sawtooth Mountains of Idaho, U.S.A., that's just what we did.

We adopted the Sawtooth Pack as pups and created a 25-acre (10-ha) home in a wild setting with plenty of room for them to roam. The wolves bonded with us and—as practical and scientific as we tried to be—we bonded with them. This connection enabled us to study and share intimate, never before seen wolf behavior with the world. With the Sawtooth Pack, it became our mission to show people that these endangered creatures are not only important to our natural world, but also intelligent, social animals, wholly devoted to one another— just like a family.

Lakota was at the very heart of the Sawtooth family. Though he grew to be the largest member of the group, he ended up at the very bottom of the social order—a position called the omega. Being an omega wolf is tough:

Omega wolves are often bullied by higher-ranking pack members, denied food until all the others have eaten, and forced to constantly submit to other wolves.

While it was difficult to watch timid Lakota be bullied, he taught us just how important the omega role is in a wolf's world. To avoid rough treatment, it was in Lakota's best interest to keep the pack's mood light. With a quick "play bow," Lakota was often the one to start a fun game of tag. And by submitting to the other wolves, he reduced tension and fighting. Lakota's games also strengthened bonds within the pack, which are important to maintain in a close-knit family. Still, the bullying was often hard for Lakota to take. But soon, Matsi, the pack's high-ranking beta, or second-in-command, stood up for Lakota when the going got tough. Through their friendship, Lakota developed a confidence that allowed him to overcome his omega status and make a lifelong friend.

Want to learn more about wolves?

WEBSITES

animals.nationalgeographic.com/animals/mammals/wolf
Fact page and range map from National Geographic

kids.nationalgeographic.com/content/kids/en_US/animals/gray-wolf
Fact page, photos, and range map from National Geographic Kids

livingwithwolves.org
Site for Jim and Jamie Dutcher's foundation dedicated to raising public awareness about wolves and revealing their true nature

natgeoed.org/gray-wolf-educator-guide
natgeoed.org/gray-wolf-family-guide
Educational guides from National Geographic about gray wolves and the Dutchers' work with the Sawtooth Pack that include hands-on activities for families and teachers

nps.gov/yell/naturescience/wolves.htm
Learn about the wolves of Yellowstone National Park

wolfquest.org
Wildlife simulation game from the Minnesota Zoo that teaches wolf behavior and ecology

BOOKS

Brandenburg, Jim. *Face to Face With Wolves*. National Geographic Society, 2010.

Dutcher, Jim, and Jamie Dutcher. *The Hidden Life of Wolves*. National Geographic Society, 2013.

——. *Living With Wolves*. The Mountaineers Books, 2005.

——. *Wolves at Our Door*. Pocket Books, 2002.

George, Jean Craighead. *The Wolves Are Back*. Dutton Juvenile, 2008.

Jazynka, Kitson. *Mission Wolf Rescue*. National Geographic Society, 2014.

Marsh, Laura. *National Geographic Readers: Wolves*. National Geographic Society, 2012.

Simon, Seymour. *Wolves*. HarperCollins, 2009.

PLACES TO SEE WOLVES

In the United States

Brookfield Zoo, 8400 31st Street, Brookfield, Illinois

Cheyenne Mountain Zoo, 4250 Cheyenne Mountain Zoo Road, Colorado Springs, Colorado

Cleveland Metroparks Zoo, 3900 Wildlife Way, Cleveland, Ohio

Smithsonian National Zoo, 3001 Connecticut Avenue NW, Washington, D.C.

Woodland Park Zoo, 750 N. 50th Street, Seattle, Washington

Yellowstone National Park Idaho, Montana, Wyoming

Around the World

Dublin Zoo, Dublin, Ireland

Taipei Zoo, Taipei, Taiwan

Tiergarten Schönbrunn, Vienna, Austria

Ueno Zoo, Tokyo, Japan

Zoo Basel, Basel, Switzerland

LET'S STOP BULLYING

To learn more about bullying and prevention, grab a parent and visit stopbullying.gov or stompoutbullying.org. Also visit natgeo.com/kids/friend for an important guide to developing friendships.

Credits

For our grandchildren, Arianna, Sofia, Natalie, Sebastian, and children all around the world. Together we can make a difference for wolves and the natural world. The future is in your hands.
—Jim and Jamie Dutcher

All photos by Jim and Jamie Dutcher unless otherwise noted: Cover (mountains): IDAK/Shutterstock; cover flap (author photo): Garrick Dutcher; 32 (LO): National Museum of the American Indian, Smithsonian Institute (13/7839), photo by Katherine Fogden.

STAFF FOR THIS BOOK

Kate Olesin, *Project Editor*
Callie Broaddus, *Art Director*
Hillary Leo, *Photo Editor*
Carl Mehler, *Director of Maps*
Elizabeth Carney, *Contributing Writer*
Dr. Jeffrey Means, *Expert Consultant*
Paige Towler, *Editorial Assistant*
Sanjida Rashid and Rachel Kenny, *Design Production Assistants*
Colm McKeveny, *Rights Clearance Specialist*
Michael Libonati, *Special Projects Assistant*
Grace Hill, *Managing Editor*
Michael O'Connor, *Production Editor*
Lewis R. Bassford, *Production Manager*
George Bounelis, *Manager, Production Services*
Susan Borke, *Legal and Business Affairs*

PUBLISHED BY THE NATIONAL GEOGRAPHIC SOCIETY

Gary E. Knell, *President and CEO*
John M. Fahey, *Chairman of the Board*
Melina Gerosa Bellows, *Chief Education Officer*
Declan Moore, *Chief Media Officer*
Hector Sierra, *Senior Vice President and General Manager, Book Division*

SENIOR MANAGEMENT TEAM, KIDS PUBLISHING AND MEDIA

Nancy Laties Feresten, *Senior Vice President;* Jennifer Emmett, *Vice President, Editorial Director, Kids Books;* Julie Vosburgh Agnone, *Vice President, Editorial Operations;* Rachel Buchholz, *Editor and Vice President,* NG Kids *magazine;* Michelle Sullivan, *Vice President, Kids Digital;* Eva Absher-Schantz, *Design Director;* Jay Sumner, *Photo Director;* Hannah August, *Marketing Director;* R. Gary Colbert, *Production Director*

DIGITAL Anne McCormack, *Director;* Laura Goertzel, Sara Zeglin, *Producers;* Emma Rigney, *Creative Producer;* Bianca Bowman, *Assistant Producer;* Natalie Jones, *Senior Product Manager*

The National Geographic Society is one of the world's largest nonprofit scientific and educational organizations. Founded in 1888 to "increase and diffuse geographic knowledge," the Society's mission is to inspire people to care about the planet. It reaches more than 400 million people worldwide each month through its official journal, *National Geographic,* and other magazines; National Geographic Channel; television documentaries; music; radio; films; books; DVDs; maps; exhibitions; live events; school publishing programs; interactive media; and merchandise. National Geographic has funded more than 10,000 scientific research, conservation, and exploration projects and supports an education program promoting geographic literacy.

For more information, please visit nationalgeographic.com, call 1-800-NGS LINE (647-5463), or write to the following address:
National Geographic Society
1145 17th Street N.W.
Washington, D.C. 20036-4688 U.S.A.

Visit us online at nationalgeographic.com/books

For librarians and teachers: ngchildrensbooks.org

More for kids from National Geographic:
kids.nationalgeographic.com

For information about special discounts for bulk purchases, please contact National Geographic Books Special Sales: ngspecsales@ngs.org

For rights or permissions inquiries, please contact National Geographic Books Subsidiary Rights: ngbookrights@ngs.org

Lakota doll with cradleboard, circa 1890

A NOTE ON THE DESIGN

Lakota was named after a word in the Lakota Sioux language, so much of the imagery in this book is inspired by Lakota Sioux culture. Native American designs vary in color, pattern, and beadwork among different tribes and regions. The colors in this book reflect the beadwork shown on the pictured Lakota Sioux doll, and the borders echo patterns found in traditional beadwork. In addition, the vegetation silhouetted throughout are lodgepole pine and juniper trees, commonly found in Lakota's home in the Sawtooth Mountains.

Trade hardcover ISBN: 978-1-4263-2082-8
Reinforced library binding ISBN: 978-1-4263-2083-5

Printed in Hong Kong
15/THK/1